Cambridge **Discovery Education**™
▶ **INTERACTIVE READERS**

Series editor: Bob Hastings

ROBOTS
THE NEXT GENERATION?

B2+

Caroline Shackleton and Nathan Paul Turner

CAMBRIDGE
UNIVERSITY PRESS

DISCOVERY
EDUCATION™

CAMBRIDGE
UNIVERSITY PRESS

University Printing House, Cambridge CB2 8BS, United Kingdom

Cambridge University Press is part of the University of Cambridge.

It furthers the University's mission by disseminating knowledge in the pursuit of education, learning and research at the highest international levels of excellence.

www.cambridge.org
Information on this title: www.cambridge.org/9781107677623

First published 2014
3rd printing 2015

Printed in Hong Kong, China, by Golden Cup Printing Company Limited

A catalog record for this publication is available from the British Library.

Library of Congress Cataloging-in-Publication Data

Shackleton, Caroline.
  Robots : the next generation? : level B2+ / Caroline Shackleton and Nathan Paul Turner.
    pages cm. -- (Cambridge discovery interactive readers)
  ISBN 978-1-107-67762-3 (pbk. : alk. paper)
1. Robots--Juvenile literature. 2. English language--Textbooks for foreign speakers. 3. Readers (Elementary) I. Title.

TJ211.2.S52 2014
629.8'92--dc23

                              2013016895

ISBN 978-1-107-67762-3

Additional resources for this publication at www.cambridge.org

Layout services, art direction, book design, and photo research: Q2ABillSMITH GROUP
Editorial services: Hyphen S.A.
Audio production: CityVox, New York
Video production: Q2ABillSMITH GROUP

Contents

Before You Read:
Get Ready!

Robots have been part of our lives for many years. Today, they can do all kinds of things: clean our houses, protect soldiers, and gather information during an emergency. Who knows what things they'll be able to do in the future?

Words to Know

Complete the definitions with the correct words.

mechanism   humanoid   craftsman   remote-controlled

1 _____: describes a machine that is operated from a distance using electrical or radio signals

2 _____: a person with a skill at making things

3 _____: a machine with the appearance or qualities of a human

4 _____: a part of a machine or a set of parts that work together

Words to Know

Read the paragraph. Then complete the definitions with the correct highlighted words.

New innovations in robot technology are blurring the differences between humans and machines. This may mean we will soon see autonomous machines capable of thinking and making their own decisions. Until recently, robots have been able to work with extreme precision in environments such as car factories. This work, however, is programmed by humans. Many people refuse to accept that a machine will ever have a spirit or mind similar to our own.

1 _____ : a part of a person – their feelings and character – that many people believe to be separate from the body

2 _____ : changes and new ideas

3 _____ : exactness and accuracy in form and detail

4 _____ : able to do things independently

5 _____ : becoming unclear

? EVALUATE

How are robots presently used? Check your answers as you read.

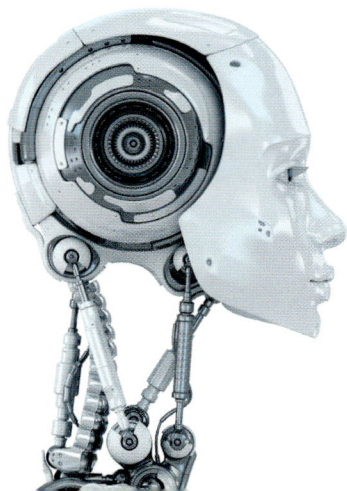
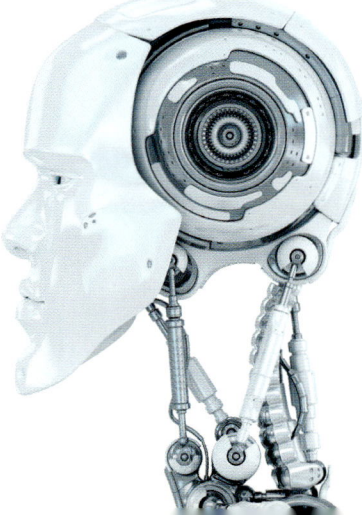

Eighteenth-century
Karakuri dolls from Japan

CHAPTER 1

Robots and Japan

IF IN THE FUTURE YOU BUY A HOUSEHOLD ROBOT, THE CHANCES ARE IT WILL BE JAPANESE.

Japan is famous for its long tradition of automatons, or machines that look and act like humans. In the 18th and 19th centuries, realistic human models, known as *Karakuri ningyō*, or "dolls that trick," were seen in homes, theaters, and religious ceremonies. The most common example was a small model of a woman in a kimono that served cups of tea to guests.

These **sophisticated** dolls became highly popular. Interestingly, the great engineer Tanaka Hisashige, founder[1] of the company that would eventually become TOSHIBA, actually started his career in the early 19th century as a maker of *Karakuri* dolls.

[1] **founder:** someone who begins a business or company

But Japan did not invent automatons. In fact, they have been with us for thousands of years. The word automaton comes from the Greek "it moves itself." The 1st-century Greek inventor Hero was famous for his automated machines, which included moving dancers and fountains.

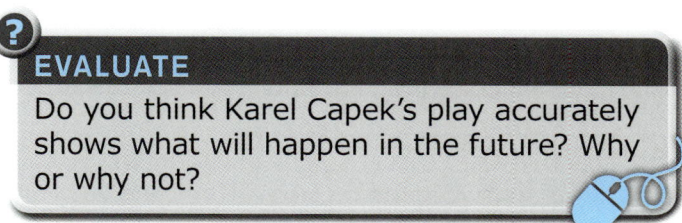

Hero's automatic theater

There are also many stories from ancient China of wooden automatons that sang, danced, or served drinks. Later, in the 12th century, the Islamic scholar Al-Jazarī wrote a whole book on mechanisms and automatons, which included clocks, animals, a waitress, and even a programmable musical band complete with flute-player and drummer!

The English word robot comes from the Czech language and means "to serve." It was first used in the 1920s in a play by the Czech writer Karel Capek, titled *R.U.R.* (Rossum's Universal Robots). The play showed a futuristic world where human-like machines did all the work. In Capek's play these machines could think and feel, and eventually they rebelled[2] against their human **rulers**.

[2] **rebel:** not follow rules

?

EVALUATE

Do you think Karel Capek's play accurately shows what will happen in the future? Why or why not?

By the 1920s in Japan robots were starting to appear in department stores. At first, however, they were not much more than complicated Karakuri.

The first Japanese humanoid robot was created in 1928 and was called *Gakutensoku*, or "Learning from the Laws of Nature." It was a Buddha-like model that used air to move its head and hands.

Its creator, the biologist Makoto Nishimura, believed these machines were part of nature. He is quoted as saying, "If one considers humans as the children of nature, artificial humans created by the hand of man are thus nature's grandchildren." His robot became a huge success and toured Asia and Europe.

Nishimura's opinions highlight the Japanese attitude to machines and technology and the fascination they have with robots. This may be linked to Japan's Shinto religion, whose followers regard all things as having spirits. Tools and all objects made with tools possess their own special

qualities, almost as if they were individuals. Certainly the Japanese view of robots is very different from the views traditionally held in Western cultures, which are often suspicious of robots.

Gakutensoku and Makoto Nishimura (left), 1928

The Japanese look upon robots as things of interest and beauty, designed to help humans and make our lives better. This view was most famously expressed in the 1951 Manga comic, *Tetsuwan Atomu*. Atomu, or Astro Boy, as he was later known in the West, was the first major robot character to show robots as friendly and helpful.

Astroboy, a robot hero in comic books

The Japanese love of comic book robot characters, together with the country's fast increasing electronics industry, meant that by the 1980s Japan had become a world leader in robot research and production. Today, more than a third of the world's industrial robots work in factories in Japan.

As well as the typical industrial robots, many robots are designed simply as toys or for entertainment. Animal robots, dancing robots, car-driving robots, even piano-playing robots are all made and sold in Japan. And as technology improves, the differences between humans and machines may become increasingly blurred.

CHAPTER 2

Robots and Recreation

FOR THE JAPANESE, ROBOTS ARE A GREAT SOURCE OF ENTERTAINMENT.

Technically, a robot is any kind of autonomous self-controlled or remote-controlled machine, often used in factories for dangerous or precision work. But when we think of a robot, we often imagine a machine with a recognizably human face and figure. These robots are called androids (from the Greek for man, *andr-*) and are specifically designed to have characteristics that make them more attractive to humans.

Japan has a keen interest in humanoid models. Karakuri dolls, for example, were seen as more than models; they were respected as an art form. The Japanese fascination with robots meant that in the late 20th century, when huge improvements were being made in motors and computing, many electronics companies began to design humanoid robots that could interact with people on a social level.

The first entertainment robot with commercial success was not a humanoid, however, but a robot dog. Designed as a toy pet and **launched** in 1999, Sony's *AIBO* quickly became popular worldwide. The AIBO (Japanese for "companion") could walk, could see using cameras, and had special software that allowed it to develop from puppy to adult, learning to play and understand up to 100 voice commands. Furthermore, special programmable software allowed owners to change their AIBO's personality and behavior.

Teams of AIBOs have even played at the annual RoboCup, a soccer tournament where all the competitors must be autonomous robots.

AIBOs at the Robocup soccer tournament

ASIMO

QRIO

Humanoid robots have proved more difficult to make. However, in 2000 Honda finally introduced its first real humanoid robot, *ASIMO*.

ASIMO was able to help disabled people move around more easily. The robot could recognize and respond to human movements and commands, and was aware of its environment. It has made many public appearances, talking, dancing, and even conducting an orchestra. Its little brother, the *QRIO* made by Sony, could run and interact to such an extent that it was also capable of playing in the RoboCup.

Although the QRIO was too expensive to be produced commercially, there are now many different humanoid robots available on the market. They are generally simpler, more like expensive remote-controlled toys, but they are all humanoid and have some degree of autonomy.

The lack of easily available or reasonably-priced humanoid robots hasn't stopped Japan's robot enthusiasts. DIY[3] robotics has become increasingly popular in recent years, to such an extent that a robot championship, Robo-One, was started in 2002.

[3]**DIY:** the activity of making something yourself rather than buying it or paying for someone else to do it

The championship consists of a series of tasks that the homemade robots must perform. Tasks include falling from a standing position, getting up, walking, jumping, and even competing against other robots in a one-on-one boxing match. There has also been a Robo-One soccer match.

The robots in Robo-One are designed and built at home by individual designers, but may use commercial parts. Many robots are made from aluminum and powered by small electric motors.

One problem with two-legged robots is how to make them walk like us. Robots look awkward when they walk because they constantly **bend** their knees. However, in 2011 the Nagoya Institute of Technology produced the first robot legs modeled on human biomechanics. So naturally moving humanoids may soon be a common sight.

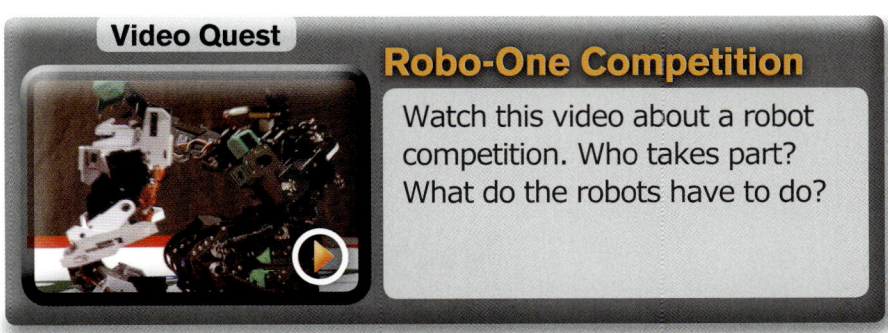

Video Quest

Robo-One Competition

Watch this video about a robot competition. Who takes part? What do the robots have to do?

Japanese craftsmanship has a long tradition.

CHAPTER 3

Robots and Money

JAPAN IS THE THIRD LARGEST ECONOMY IN THE WORLD AND HAS THE LARGEST ELECTRONICS INDUSTRY, IN WHICH IT IS CONSIDERED A LEADING INNOVATOR.

The Japanese have traditionally been noted for the high quality of their craftsmanship. European travelers arriving in Japan in the 16th and 17th century were amazed at its architecture, metalwork, and technology.

After the Second World War, the Japanese emphasis on quality and precision helped to create strong, **dynamic** industries, innovating in many areas. Japanese cars and electronics became synonymous[4] with quality, reliability, and affordability. This led to continuous economic growth for over 30 years, which leveled off in the late 20th century.

[4]**synonymous:** having the same or nearly the same meaning

Japanese cars became popular around the world in the 1970s.

As Japan enters the 21st century, the main problem its economy faces is a shortage of workers, a result of an aging population and a falling birth rate. These changes mean that, among other things, there are fewer workers to earn money or care for **the elderly**.

Many people in Japan believe that the Japanese robotics industry may be the answer to Japan's challenges, both economically (in 2010, the worldwide industry was worth $5.6 billion), but also as a technology that can produce workers and caregivers for the country's aging population.

?

ANALYZE

What qualities have helped Japan become a strong economy? What problems might the country suffer in the future?

CHAPTER 4

Robots and Work

WILL TOMORROW'S ROBOTS BE ABLE TO FULFILL A SOCIAL ROLE?

What can Japan do to solve the problem of the reduction in its workforce? Traditionally suspicious of foreigners, the country seems reluctant[5] to relax its strict immigration policy, looking instead to the robotics industry to provide its workers.

What would seem a strange solution in many other countries seems perfectly normal to the electronics-obsessed[6] Japanese. Robots in Japanese society already carry out many different roles. Here are a few ways that robots are becoming a part of everyday life in Japan.

[5]**reluctant:** not wanting to do something and therefore slow to do it
[6]**obsessed:** overly interested in or thinking about something much more than usual

Healthcare

One of the main shortages in workers in Japan at the moment is in healthcare, especially for the elderly. Although there are many trained nurses available from other parts of Asia, Japan allows very few immigrants into the country. Consequently, many robotics firms are looking at the possibility of robot nurses.

Toyota launched four robot nursing models in 2013. These machines aren't humanoid, but resemble motorized chairs, designed to help patients move around and get in and out of bed.

A highly innovative use of a robot in healthcare can be found in Tokyo's Cyberdyne gym. Here, users can exercise wearing robotic legs that recognize **impulses** made by the brain when the person wants to walk. With practice, people who have problems with their legs can walk around and do exercises.

A robot nurse

Robotic legs
at Cyberdyne

Security

Several Japanese companies have built security robots. There are robots to guard houses and offices, a robot that collects cash from banks, and a robot that can stop criminals. The Tmsuk Company's T-34 is a small, four-wheeled robot that can be controlled by mobile phone. It can catch thieves by firing a net over them.

Other robots have been used to direct traffic in Tokyo. And Fujitsu has produced a guide robot for offices and malls. It recognizes faces and has a touch screen that people can press for information.

Actroids

An astounding example of Japanese robot philosophy can be seen in their development of actroids. A combination of the words actor and android, these robots are specifically designed to look as believably human as possible.

Robot directing traffic in Japan

The HRP-4C actroid

The first actroid, presented at the 2003 International Robot Convention by the University of Osaka, was modeled on the looks of an average Japanese woman. It had realistic silicone skin and could blink,[7] speak, and breathe, using air to move its **features**.

Later models are even more realistic. Professor Ishiguro of Osaka University believes that human acceptance of robots depends on them having a familiar appearance. In the future, he hopes that these human copies could be used to represent people in business meetings and in other events. So far, the closest any of the actroids has come was when HRP-4C starred as a model in the 2009 Tokyo Fashion Week.

[7]**blink:** close and open the eyes quickly

Video Quest

Android Robots

Watch this video about android robots. How did the professor make the robot? How does he use the robot?

CHAPTER 5

Robots and Life

JAPAN'S RELIGIOUS TRADITIONS HELP ITS PEOPLE APPRECIATE ROBOTS.

Mindless metal boxes, coldly following their programming to the end, robots are not to be trusted.

This, at least, is the impression you might get from many Hollywood movies. Traditionally, robots in Hollywood have generally played the bad guy, an unforgiving, unstoppable creature of incredible power, usually only defeated because of its lack of flexibility and imagination. From movies like *Blade Runner* and *Terminator* to *The Matrix*, we are often shown a world where, given the opportunity, robots and computers will enslave humans and try to take over.

This view reflects a deep mistrust of machines in Western culture, a sense of separation from the things we create. However, it is a view not necessarily shared by other cultures. In Japan, many fictional accounts of robots are positive. Robots are seen as a force for good, as creators of a more pleasant society.

These different points of view carry over into everyday life. An American may see robots as a threat to his or her job, as an unnecessary complication, or simply as a useless toy. In Japan the same robot would be seen as a way to make work easier and more efficient, and as an interesting companion, as something fun. This probably explains why there are hundreds of humanoid robots being developed in Japan, while in the USA there are currently just two.

So why is there such a difference between these two points of view? Many people have written about the subject, both in Japan and abroad. It seems mainly to be a question of whether and how much something is seen to be alive. In this respect, Japan's Shinto and Buddhist heritage[8] plays an important role.

....

[8]**heritage:** the history, traditions, and things that belong to the culture of a particular society, such as languages, ceremonies, or buildings

Shinto involves the worship of Kami.

Japan's Religious Tradition

While Buddhism and Shinto are officially separate, in reality most people practice them together. Buddhism, with its belief in the oneness or unity of all things, was imported from China. Shinto is a set of religious beliefs and practices native to Japan and was first recorded in the 8th century.

Shinto involves the worship[9] of *Kami*, which roughly translates as "spirits." These spirits can be a natural experience, such as wind or rain, or the spirit of a natural place, such as a forest or river, or even rocks. This recognition of spiritual life in all things and actions is known as animism. Although Kami can also be the spirits of ancestors or people, they are not gods in the Western sense of the word.

[9]**worship:** praying to a god

Shinto's main aim is to keep in harmony[10] with the surrounding world by showing respect for the kami that inhabit it. In the same way, the tools you use or works you create possess their own spirit or identity, something worthy of respect. It is not surprising that such a belief would give rise to a culture of exceptional craftsmen.

A Sense of Connection

This sense of connection with the things an artist or designer creates is very different from Western ideas, which sharply divide living, thinking beings from lifeless machines. Japanese craftsmen's natural respect for and appreciation of the machines they create becomes even stronger when applied to a responsive robot.

In Japan, robots are not seen only as tools that exist to make human life easier. As one writer has put it, it is no longer a question of robots doing things for people, but of doing things with them. This is a philosophy that looks into a future where man and machine live in harmony.

....

[10] **harmony:** agreement of ideas, feelings, or actions

Video Quest

Religion in Japan

Watch this video about the Ainu people of Japan. How are their beliefs related to Shinto?

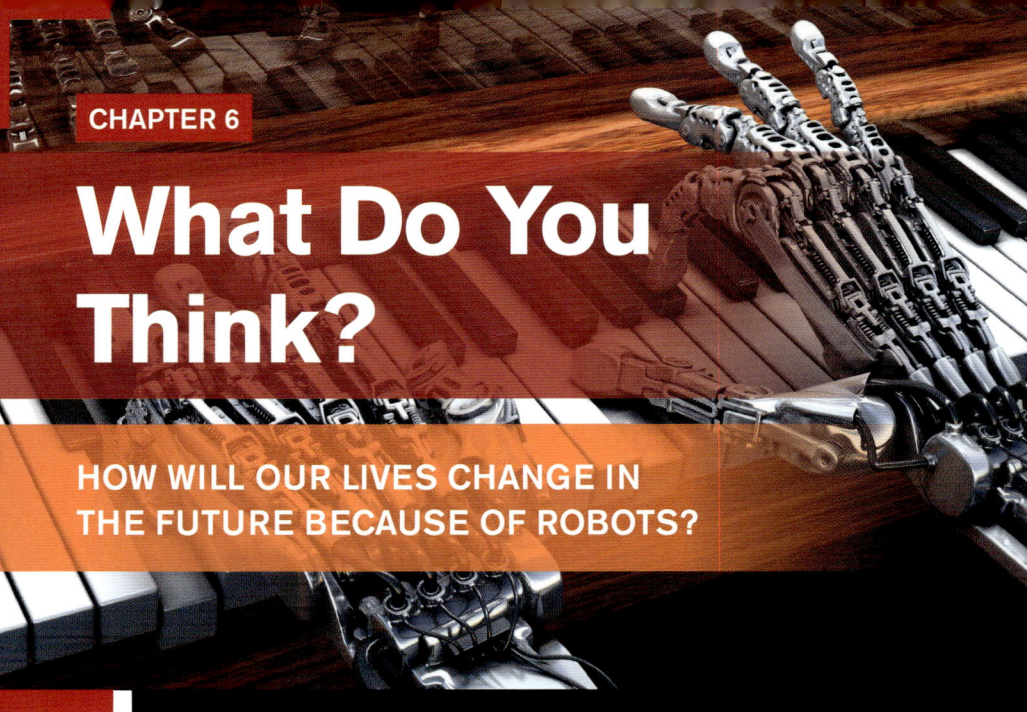

CHAPTER 6

What Do You Think?

HOW WILL OUR LIVES CHANGE IN THE FUTURE BECAUSE OF ROBOTS?

Every year, technological advances mean newer, faster computers, newer communication devices, and more sophisticated, more capable robots.

In Japan, this is viewed with excitement. Perhaps, due to their philosophical history, the Japanese are more capable of "understanding" and working with robots. Do you think robots will become as popular in other parts of the world? Will they be as accepted in other countries or will they be objects of fear?

Robots will probably soon play a more important role in our lives. They will be able to move around better and perform simple jobs around the house, such as painting, cleaning, and other household tasks. But will they be able to communicate with humans, have decision-making abilities, and generally live alongside us on the planet?

The robot brain is based on computers and their increasing ability to carry out billions of instructions very quickly. But will robot brains ever have the same kind of intelligence as humans do? Will the computer-based artificial brain allow robots to become like intelligent human beings?

Some predictions say "Yes!" Already computers can "understand" humans to some extent by recognizing our speech. Can you imagine having a robot as a friend? Will children go to school with robot friends who help them with their homework?

How will people behave socially with robots in the future? Will they be treated as machines? Or will they act so like us that we treat them as equals? Will we have to change our laws to include the fair treatment of robots? We might even have groups fighting for "robot rights." For example, should robots be paid for the work they do? And if so, how?

What do you think will happen? And will it happen in your lifetime?

After You Read

Read the following sentences and choose Ⓐ, Ⓑ, or Ⓒ.

1 What does the word "robot" mean?

- Ⓐ A machine with legs.
- Ⓑ A machine that does work.
- Ⓒ A toy that plays games.

2 How do the Japanese view robots?

- Ⓐ as unintelligent tools
- Ⓑ as threatening monsters
- Ⓒ as useful companions

3 What form did the earliest computerized robot toy take?

- Ⓐ a doll
- Ⓑ an animal
- Ⓒ a woman

4 Why are humanoid robots not presently mass produced?

- Ⓐ Because they cost a lot to make.
- Ⓑ Because they take a long time to make.
- Ⓒ Because they are not popular enough.

5 What is the biggest difficulty for people who make robots as a hobby?

- Ⓐ creating life-like movement
- Ⓑ getting the right pieces
- Ⓒ affording the electronics

6 What is one of the main economic problems in Japan nowadays?

- Ⓐ its taxes
- Ⓑ its inflation
- Ⓒ its workforce

7 Why are Western countries' opinions of robots more negative than Japan's?

- Ⓐ because of Hollywood films
- Ⓑ because of different cultural beliefs
- Ⓒ because of unemployment

Match

Match the information with the following four chapters from the book. Which chapter refers to each of these ideas?

A	B	C	D
Chapter one Robots and Japan	Chapter two Robots and Recreation	Chapter three Robots and Money	Chapter four Robots and Work

1 People making robots at home as a hobby _____

2 The work of a famous electronics company owner _____

3 Robots helping to fight crime _____

4 Problems taking care of Japan's elderly _____

5 A relationship with an artificial pet _____

6 Robots participating in business meetings _____

7 A robotic cartoon character _____

8 The quality of Japanese vehicles _____

?

ANALYZE

Robots do important jobs in Japan. Can you think of other professions that could use robots? What work could they do?

Job	Possible tasks

Answer Key

Words to Know, page 4

1 remote-controlled **2** craftsman **3** humanoid
4 mechanism

Words to Know, page 5

1 spirit **2** innovations **3** precision **4** autonomous
5 blurring

Evaluate, page 5
Answers will vary.

Evaluate, page 7
Answers will vary.

Video Quest, page 13
Suggested Answers: amateurs and electronics technicians;
They fight and do other things to impress the judges.

Analyze, page 15
Suggested Answers: craftsmanship, good quality products,
attention to detail/precision, a shortage of workers

Video Quest, page 19
Suggested Answers: He made a copy of his face using
sensors; He uses remote control to send the robot to give
lectures and attend meetings.

Video Quest, page 23
Shinto comes from Ainu beliefs.

Choose the Correct Answers, page 26
1 B **2** C **3** B **4** A **5** A **6** C **7** B

Match, page 27
1 B **2** A **3** D **4** C **5** B **6** D **7** A **8** C

Analyze, page 27
Answers will vary.